THE AMERICAN LANDSCAPE

GREAT BASIN

DWAYNE HICKS

PowerKiDS press

Published in 2026 by The Rosen Publishing Group, Inc.
2544 Clinton Street, Buffalo, NY 14224

First Edition

Editor: Greg Roza
Book Design: Michael Flynn

Photo Credits: Cover, p. 1 Arlene Waller/Shutterstock.com; (series background) Omeris/Shutterstock.com; p. 5 Traveller70/Shutterstock.com; p. 7 Rainer Lesniewski/Shutterstock.com; p. 9 D. Lillie Photography/Shutterstock.com; p. 11 Zack Frank/Shutterstock.com; p. 13 (Joshua tree) Oleg Kovtun Hydrobio/Shutterstock.com; p. 13 (bristlecone pine) Cavan-Images/Shutterstock.com; p. 13 (cactus) Al Bittler/Shutterstock.com; p. 15 Dennis W Donohue/Shutterstock.com; p. 17 Dominic Gentilcore PhD/Shutterstock.com; p. 19 Zack Frank/Shutterstock.com; p. 21 Ventu Photo/Shutterstock.com.

Library of Congress Cataloging-in-Publication Data

Names: Hicks, Dwayne, author.
Title: Great Basin / Dwayne Hicks.
Description: Buffalo : PowerKids Press, [2025] | Series: The American landscape | Includes index.
Identifiers: LCCN 2024044850 (print) | LCCN 2024044851 (ebook) | ISBN 9781499450835 (library binding) | ISBN 9781499450828 (paperback) | ISBN 9781499450842 (ebook)
Subjects: LCSH: Great Basin–Juvenile literature.
Classification: LCC E78.G67 H535 2025 (print) | LCC E78.G67 (ebook) | DDC 979–dc23/eng/20241024
LC record available at https://lccn.loc.gov/2024044850
LC ebook record available at https://lccn.loc.gov/2024044851

Manufactured in China

CPSIA Compliance Information: Batch #QSPK26. For Further Information contact Rosen Publishing at 1-800-237-9932.

CONTENTS

Discovering the Great Basin

A basin is an area, or piece of land, where water doesn't flow out. Instead, water forms lakes and **swamps** within the basin. Some of these lakes are seasonal. The Great Basin is one of the largest basins in the world. There's so much to discover at the Great Basin!

Where in the World?

The Great Basin is in the western United States. It covers most of Nevada and half of Utah. The two largest cities in this area are Salt Lake City, Utah, and Reno, Nevada. Much of the water in the Great Basin flows into the Great Salt Lake in Utah.

Oregon
Idaho
Great Basin
Great Salt Lake
Reno
Salt Lake City
Nevada
California
Utah
Death Valley
Mojave Desert
Arizona

So Much to See!

The Great Basin has long mountains and flat valleys. It also has deserts, caves, and smaller basins. The area around the Great Salt Lake is a large **salt flat**. Some areas have beautiful **landforms** such as **arches**. Death Valley is the lowest and hottest place in the Unites States!

Lexington Arch

Deserts, Mountains, and Rain

Most of the Great Basin is a desert. Death Valley gets as little as 2.1 inches (5.3 cm) of rain a year. Mountainous areas commonly get up to 50 inches (127 cm) of rain a year. Mountains also get snow in the winter.

Basin Plants

At lower **elevations**, the Great Basin has plants commonly found in deserts. This **includes** Joshua trees, cactuses, and bushes. At higher elevation, forests are more common. These include mahogany and bristlecone pine trees. You will see different kinds of wildflowers in different seasons and elevations.

Joshua tree
bristlecone pine
cactus

Basin Animals

Animals at lower elevations include those commonly found in deserts. They include snakes, lizards, bugs, small **mammals**, and wild horses. Birds and fish live closer to—or in—bodies of water. At higher elevations, you will find bighorn sheep, mule deer, rabbits, porcupines, mice, and much more.

Native Americans

Native Americans have lived in the Great Basin for thousands of years. Some of the groups left rock art that we can still see today. Many of these groups **roamed** in search of food. Native Americans that still call the Great Basin home are the Shoshone, Ute, Paiute, and Washoe.

Moving West

European Americans first started settling in the Great Basin in the 1800s. Many got there following the Oregon Trail. More people arrived during the California Gold Rush in 1848. In 1869, the first cross-country railroad was finished. This allowed the towns and cities of the Great Basin to grow.

Visiting the Great Basin

Today, people visit the Great Basin for many reasons. Visitors can walk trails, camp, fish, and much more. Guides teach visitors all about the area and Native people who live there. Some people drive cars on the salt flats. You can even walk inside a cave!

GLOSSARY

arch: A curved stone structure that can be walked under.

elevation: Height above sea level.

include: To have as part of a whole group.

landform: A natural feature of an area of land.

mammal: Any warm-blooded animal whose babies drink milk and whose body is covered with hair or fur.

roam: To move from place to place.

salt flat: A large, flat area of land covered with salt, left over from a body of salt water that dried up long ago.

swamp: Wet, soft land often partly covered with water.

FOR MORE INFORMATION

BOOKS

Enz, Tammy. *Science on the Oregon Trail*. Mankato, MN: Capstone Press, 2022.

O'Mara, John. *The Shoshone*. Buffalo, NY: Enslow Publishing, 2022.

Quick, Megan. *Do You Dare Visit Death Valley?* Buffalo, NY: Enslow Publishing, 2024.

WEBSITES

Kiddle: Great Basin Facts for Kids
kids.kiddle.co/Great_Basin
Read more about the Great Basin at this informative website.

National Geographic Kids: Native People of the American Great Basin
kids.nationalgeographic.com/history/article/native-people-of-the-american-great-basin
This website includes a short history of the Indigenous People who have lived in the Great Basin.

INDEX